D1377494

Slugs and Snails

By Theresa Greenaway

Photographs by Chris Fairclough

RSVP

RAINTREE
STECK-VAUGHN
PUBLISHERS

A Steck-Vaughn Company

Austin, Texas

Published by Raintree Steck-Vaughn Publishers, an imprint of Steck-Vaughn Company.

Acknowledgments
Project Editors: Gianna Williams, Kathy DeVico
Project Manager: Joyce Spicer
Illustrator: Jim Chanell
Design: Ian Winton

Planned and produced by Discovery Books Limited

Library of Congress Cataloging-in-Publication Data
Greenaway, Theresa, 1947–
Slugs and snails/by Theresa Greenaway; photographs by Chris Fairclough.
p. cm. — (Minipets)
Includes bibliographical references (p. 30) and index.
Summary: Provides information on the identification, life cycle, and habitats of slugs and snails, as well as on how to collect and care for them as pets.
ISBN 0-8172-5587-7 (hardcover)
ISBN 0-8172-4207-4 (softcover)
1. Slugs (Mollusks) as pets — Juvenile literature. 2. Snails as pets — Juvenile literature. 3. Slugs (Mollusks) — Juvenile literature. 4. Snails — Juvenile literature.
[1. Slugs (Mollusks) as pets. 2. Snails as pets. 3. Slugs (Mollusks).
4. Snails. 5. Pets.] I. Fairclough, Chris, ill. II. Title.
III. Series: Greenaway, Theresa, 1947– Minipets.
SF459.S48G74   1999
639' .4838 — dc21
98-34070
CIP   AC

1 2 3 4 5 6 7 8 9 0 LB 02 01 00 99 98
Printed and bound in the United States of America.

Words explained in the glossary appear in **bold** the first time they are used in the text.

Contents

Keeping Slugs and Snails

Slow-moving, slimy slugs and snails are not everyone's choice for pets. But they are very interesting creatures, as you will discover when you start watching them. Before you bring these "pets" into your home, you will need to ask your parents' permission.

▶ Remember to wash your hands after handling your minipets.

Animal or tropical fruit?

This large banana slug can grow up to 10 inches (25 cm) long. Native to the northwestern United States, it eats all kinds of living and decaying plants.

Slugs and snails belong to a group of animals called mollusks. They have soft, legless bodies. Snails make hard, **whorled** shells that their bodies can fit inside. Slugs are really snails without shells. But a few kinds of slugs have the remains of tiny shells on their backs.

Slugs and snails move along on a flat, slimy "foot."
Scientists call them gastropods, which means
"stomach-feet." Their head is at the front end of
the foot. Slugs and snails have four tentacles, or
feelers, that can be drawn back inside the head.

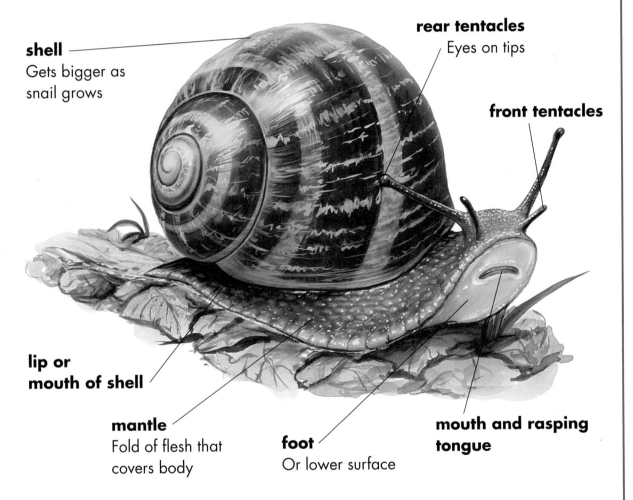

shell
Gets bigger as
snail grows

rear tentacles
Eyes on tips

front tentacles

**lip or
mouth of shell**

mantle
Fold of flesh that
covers body

foot
Or lower surface

**mouth and rasping
tongue**

Most slugs and snails have eyes at the tips of the
two longest feelers. The shorter feelers are for
smelling food. Underneath the head is the mouth.
When a snail wants to move, its head and foot come
out of the shell, but its **vital organs** stay inside.

Finding Slugs and Snails

There are many different kinds of slugs and snails—and plenty of them, as any gardener will tell you! Slugs and snails tend to live in damp places, such as ponds, riversides, and cool, moist spots in wooded areas. Gardens have lots of tasty leaves for slugs and snails to eat.

Slime and froth

Although we may find their sticky slime disgusting, it is vital to slugs and snails. Slime helps keep their bodies from drying out. It also prevents some animals and birds from eating them, because many **predators** do not like the slime sticking to their faces. Snails may produce a mass of froth when they are attacked. Slugs have stickier slime than snails.

Slugs and snails hide when it is warm and sunny. They come out when it is cool and damp, especially in the evening after a shower of rain. They are easy to find. All you need is a flashlight.

Some snails like water. Look carefully in a pond (make sure you have an adult with you). Can you see any pond snails climbing slowly up the water plants?

At the seashore, try looking in tide pools. Sea snails have different names, such as whelks or periwinkles. These snails often hide under seaweed, so lift some up and look carefully underneath.

▼ This is a great ramshorn snail that lives in ponds. Great ramshorn snails are normally dark brown, so this red one is quite unusual.

Slug and Snail Collecting

Slugs and snails move very slowly, so collecting them is easy. You will need some jars or plastic containers with airholes in the lids. Stick a blank label onto each container, so that you can write the name of your catch. Make sure you have a pencil, a small, soft paintbrush, a flat ice pop stick or plastic spoon, and a notebook.

Unless you live in a very damp area, you will find slugs and snails most easily if you look during the evening after a shower of rain.

Large snails can be picked up by their shells. Tiny snails have thin, fragile shells, so pick them up gently by rolling them onto a leaf with your paintbrush. Some snails are tiny, even when they are fully grown. Slug slime is sticky, so use the ice pop stick or spoon to lift any slugs.

Put the larger slugs and snails into your biggest containers, together with a little bit of the plant they were eating. Use smaller containers for tiny slugs and snails. Write down when and where you found your new pets, and what they were eating.

A small net is useful for collecting pond snails. Put the pond snails straight into a jar of pond water with some pondweed. Sea snails collected from tide pools must be kept in seawater, or they will die.

Identifying Your Minipets

To see which kinds of slugs and snails you have collected, you will need a hand lens, a ruler, and a notebook. A hand lens is also useful for examining your slugs and snails, especially the tiny ones. Books on slugs and snails, seashells, pond life, and even gardening books can contain information on how to identify your new pets.

To identify a slug or snail, first take some notes. How big is it? Measure the snail's shell and the length of its outstretched body. What color is it? Is there a pattern on its shell or body? If it is a snail, what shape is its shell? Some snails have flat, coiled shells. Others have rounded spirals or tall, pointed spirals. Many snails can be identified by their shells alone.

Make a collection of empty shells. You will find lots of shells washed up on the beach. Not all of them will be snails' shells, though.

Make sure the shells you collect are empty. Then carefully wash and dry them, or they will start to smell. It is important to keep a record of each shell and take notes about it in your notebook.

Beautiful sea snails
Many tropical snail shells have bright colors and interesting shapes. But even in cooler parts of the world you can find shells speckled with reds and purples, and periwinkles that may have brown, green, or even bright yellow shells.

Try to match your slugs and snails with pictures in books. Ask an adult to help you check details of color and size.

Slug and Snail Homes

You will need to make homes for your slugs and snails. Glass jars are fine for the smaller animals. Put a little bit of soil and a small tuft of grass at the bottom of each jar. Place a lid or some plastic wrap over the jar. Don't forget to make airholes so that the slug or snail can breathe.

For bigger slugs and snails, you will need a large, see-through container with a lid, such as an aquarium. Put 2 to 3 inches (5 to 8 cm) of soil in the bottom. Then add a layer of **leaf litter**.

Plant small tufts of grass and little plants in the soil, and make shelters out of flowerpots or pieces of tile. Try to make this new home similar to the natural surroundings in which you found your slugs and snails. Sprinkle the soil with water to make it moist. Put the lid on the container. Make sure it is not left in direct sunshine.

Pond snails will be happy in a small aquarium with plenty of pondweed. Put a layer of sand or gravel at the bottom of the aquarium, and slowly fill it with pond water. Keep it somewhere light, or the pondweed will die. However, do not let it get too warm.

Seawater soon becomes stale when kept in a container. Do not keep sea snails longer than a few hours, unless you live near the ocean and can change their water every day.

Caring for Slugs and Snails

Common slugs and snails are easy to look after. Nearly all kinds eat living or dead plants. Put little piles of different things—lettuce, potato peels, cake crumbs, an apple core—into their containers, and see which type of food each animal likes best.

Slugs and snails feel safer in dim light. They will not come out to feed in the bright sunlight. Remove uneaten food after a day or so. Otherwise it will grow mold.

Watch how slugs and snails use their tentacles to find food. Waving its tentacles gently, the slug or snail picks up the scent of the food and starts to glide slowly toward it. Occasionally it stops to test the air again, to make sure it is going in the right direction. Use your hand lens to watch it eat.

Slugs and snails feed using long, rough tongues called radulas. The radula is covered with rows of tiny, hard teeth. These teeth scrape the surface of the food and file off fragments, which are swallowed.

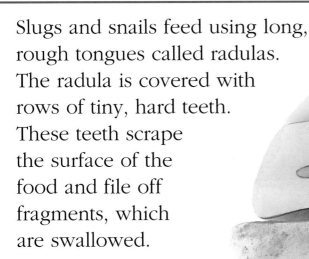

radula

A snail's shell is mostly made up of chalky material. The snail gets this from the small amounts of chalk or limestone rocks that **dissolve** in rainwater and wash into the soil. The snail swallows some of this limy or chalky water. It then **recycles** the dissolved lime and turns it back into a hard material— its shell.

▶ Many toadstools are poisonous to people. But they do not harm slugs, such as this leopard slug.

Slug and Snail Behavior

Slugs and snails are fascinating animals to watch. Try putting them on some glass. Look through the glass to see how they glide along. Inside each foot are bands of muscles. These **contract**, one after the other, so that a wave runs along the foot. This moves the animal forward, little by little. Can you see the muscles moving?

Slugs and snails cannot see clearly with their tiny eyes, but they can tell the difference between bright and dim light. Watch what happens when you shine a bright light on a slug or snail. See how your pets respond when you gently touch different parts of their bodies with a feather or blade of grass. Record the results of your experiments in your notebook.

After feeding, slugs and snails rest in a sheltered place out of sight of enemies. To find out if snails return to the same shelters, mark their shells with dots of waterproof paint or nail polish. You can do this with your pet snails, or you can mark others living in your backyard.

Silver trails

Glands just below the head of a slug or snail produce a lot of thick **mucus**. The animal moves along on this ribbon of slime, which protects its soft foot from damage and allows it to cross dry surfaces. As the slime dries, it leaves a telltale silver trail.

Pets or Pests?

Most gardeners dislike slugs and snails. Not only do slugs and snails gobble up seedlings and prize vegetables, but they also ignore the weeds! This is because many weeds have defenses such as hair, tough leaves, or unpleasant tastes.

Garden plants are grown for their colorful flowers, or for their crisp, tasty leaves. As a result, these plants have lost their natural protection. Slugs and snails can feed on them easily.

▼ It is really disappointing for a gardener to discover that a snail has wrecked the blossoms of prized plants.

By now, you should be familiar with the different kinds of slugs and snails that live in your neighborhood. Can you tell which ones are garden pests, and which ones prefer to live in compost piles?

Shell crackers

Some birds have ways of separating snails from their shells, so that they can eat the soft bodies. European song thrushes hit snails on stones until the shells shatter. The limpkin and the snail hawk live in the marshes of Florida and Georgia. They have hooked beaks that they use to remove large apple snails from their shells.

In fact, slugs and snails are not really villains. Most will eat decaying plants as well as living ones. They play a key part in breaking down and recycling dead plants and leaves so that the **nutrients** they contain are released back into the soil. This activity keeps the soil healthy, which helps new plants grow.

Multiplication

Most slugs and snails are neither male nor female—they are both. But they still need to get together in pairs before they can produce the next generation. These slow-moving animals have a long courtship. They circle around and around, making a large amount of slime. As they glide around each other, they often touch.

▼ These two slugs from a rain forest in Africa take a long time to get to know each other. Before they mate, they glide around each other in a strange, slimy ritual.

After mating, both partners crawl off to lay their eggs in damp, shady places. Slugs often burrow underground to lay their eggs. Each batch contains between 25 and 50 round, white, pearly eggs. Some slugs and snails lay eggs with harder shells.

The eggs take up to 6 weeks to hatch. The hatchlings look just like miniature adults. Snails grow tiny shells before they even emerge from their eggs.

▲ A Roman snail crawls to a patch of damp earth covered with leaves to lay its eggs. If they dry out, the eggs will die.

Slugs and snails have stretchy, slimy skin that grows with them. This means that they do not need to molt. As a snail grows, it uses a part of its body, called the **mantle**, to add a new layer around the edge of its shell. The snail never grows too big to fit inside, because the shell is always growing with it.

▶ These tiny snail hatchlings have perfectly formed shells. But each shell is extremely thin and very fragile.

When Winter Comes

Slugs and snails find life difficult when the weather grows very cold. Their soft bodies are damaged by freezing temperatures. So where do they go in the winter? Try looking under flowerpots or rotting logs. If you look in a woodpile, make sure you have an adult with you.

▼ This hibernating Roman snail has been turned upside down. You can see the hard plate of dry slime that seals its shell all winter.

Snails often seal themselves into their shells with a layer of slime. The slime forms a watertight cover over the mouth of the shell. This sticks the snail to a shed floor, basement, or anywhere else that is free of frost. Slugs burrow right down into the ground, where it is too deep for the frost to reach.

Watch when an adult digs a vegetable plot in the winter. He or she may unearth some slugs. There are slugs that spend all their lives underground. Slugs and snails may take shelter or burrow into the ground to survive a hot, dry season, too.

Eating habits

A few slugs and snails are **carnivores**. They are too slow to catch fast-moving prey, so they settle for eating other slugs, snails, or earthworms.

Keeping a Record

Your notebook is an important record of your slugs and snails. It is full of your own observations, and maybe even photographs of your gastropods.

You will have learned a lot about your pets. Perhaps you know all about their likes and dislikes. But there might still be questions you would like answered. So where can you go to find out more?

GARDEN SNAIL

Found: COMPOST PILE
Date: April 13
This snail was caught in the evening, after a rainy day. It was eating some lettuce. It was 1 inch (2.5 cm) long.

My snail likes to eat apples and potato skins.

GREAT BLACK SLUG
Found: Under a flowerpot
Date: April 27

Libraries are good places to seek information. In addition to books, there are encyclopedias on CD-ROM, and the Internet. Museums with shell collections can also be good sources of information. Find out if there is a wildlife club for children in your area.

Taking a breath

Sea snails and some kinds of pond snails breathe underwater with gills that are hidden inside their bodies. Land snails and most pond snails breathe air through a hole near the edge of their shells. Slugs breathe through a hole in their side.

Whenever you notice something different about your pets, try to investigate further. One snail's shell may coil in the opposite direction to another's. Or one particular slug might be a different color from all the others. Some pond snails always come to the surface to breathe. Others do not seem to breathe at all.

Letting Them Go

If you grow fond of your pets, you might want to keep them for a long time. This is easily done with the slugs and snails you collect from your backyard. But all animals should eventually be returned to the place they were found. (If you found them in your vegetable garden, you had better check with your mom or dad first!)

Pond snails will live in a freshwater aquarium, as long as you replace the water whenever it becomes cloudy or starts to smell. If you want to keep pond snails for longer than 2 weeks, you may need to buy filters and other equipment for your aquarium.

When it is time to release the snails, take them back to their original pond. If you collected sea snails, make sure you return them to the part of the beach where you found them.

When you are releasing slugs and snails, the time of day is important. They cannot move quickly to escape from predators or the glare of the sun. The best time to let them go is on a mild, damp evening. Put them somewhere sheltered so that they can hide.

▼ A small snail is no match for a hungry beetle. The beetle can put its head right inside the shell to eat the snail.

In spite of their coats of slime, most tiny young slugs and snails are eaten by other hungry animals. Those that survive until they are fully grown stand a fair chance of living for quite a long time. The larger kinds may take up to 4 years to reach full size. A few individuals may live for 10 years or more.

Slug and Snail Facts

Slugs are often crawling with lots of tiny creatures called mites. Mites have eight legs, so they are not insects. In fact, they are related to spiders. These scurrying creatures do not seem to bother the slug at all. Scientists think that they just feed on the slug's slime.

◄ The African giant snail's shell is 8 inches (20 cm) long!

European great gray slugs have a strange courtship ritual. Each pair climbs up a bush and dangles in midair on a thick rope of slime while mating.

South Florida tree snails live in the swamplands of the Everglades in Florida. Many of them have beautifully marked shells.

► The shell of this Haitian tree snail has stripes of many different colors.

A snail's shell is made of two layers. The outer layer is made of a see-through protein and is very thin. The inner layer is thicker. It is made of chalk, with a little bit of protein.

▼ Some sea slugs are very beautiful, with brightly colored bodies. This is to warn other hungry sea creatures that these slugs are poisonous.

▶ Some snails have hairy shells. These tiny hairs are made from the thin, outermost layer of the shell.

Some sea slugs feed on corals that have stinging cells in their tentacles. When they are eaten by the sea slug, the stings pass into its skin. So any enemy that attacks the sea slug will get badly stung!

Further Reading

Bulhozer, Theres. *Life of the Snail*. Lerner, 1987.

Fisher, Enid. *Snails*. Gareth Stevens, 1996.

Olesen, Jens, and Bo Jamer. *Snail* (Stopwatch series). Silver Burdett, 1987.

Pascoe, Elaine. *Snails and Slugs*. Blackbirch, 1998.

Ross, Michael Elsohn, et al. *Snailology* (Backyard Buddies series). Lerner, 1996.

Glossary

Carnivore An animal that eats other living animals.

Contract To shorten by tensing or clenching muscles.

Dissolve To completely merge with water.

Leaf litter A layer of fallen leaves, mostly from trees.

Mantle Part of the top of the body of a slug or snail.

Mucus Slimy liquid that animals produce from various parts of their bodies.

Nutrients The chemicals that a plant needs to take from the soil in order to grow properly.

Predator An animal that hunts another animal for food.

Recycle To reuse a substance that has been used before for another purpose.

Vital organs The parts of an animal's insides necessary for it to stay alive.

Whorled Coiled around to make a spiral.

Index

The publishers would like to thank the following for their permission to reproduce photographs:
cover (snail) Robert Maier/Bruce Coleman, 4 Scott Camazine/Oxford Scientific Films, 6 Ken Preston-Mafham/Premaphotos Wildlife, 7 Felix Labhardt/Bruce Coleman, 11 Jeff Foott/Bruce Coleman, 15 Kathie Atkinson/Oxford Scientific Films, 17 M. Nimmo/Frank Lane Picture Agency, 18 K.G. Preston-Mafham/Premaphotos Wildlife, 19 Kim Taylor/Bruce Coleman, 20 Ken Preston-Mafham/Premaphotos Wildlife, 21 top Jane Burton/Bruce Coleman, 21 bottom Dieter Hagemann/Oxford Scientific Films, 22 Robert Maier/Oxford Scientific Films, 23 H. P. Frohlich/Oxford Scientific Films, 25 Ken Preston-Mafham/Premaphotos Wildlife, 27 Dr Rod Preston-Mafham/Premaphotos Wildlife, 28 James H. Carmichael/Oxford Scientific Films, 29 Howard Hall, Oxford Scientific Films.